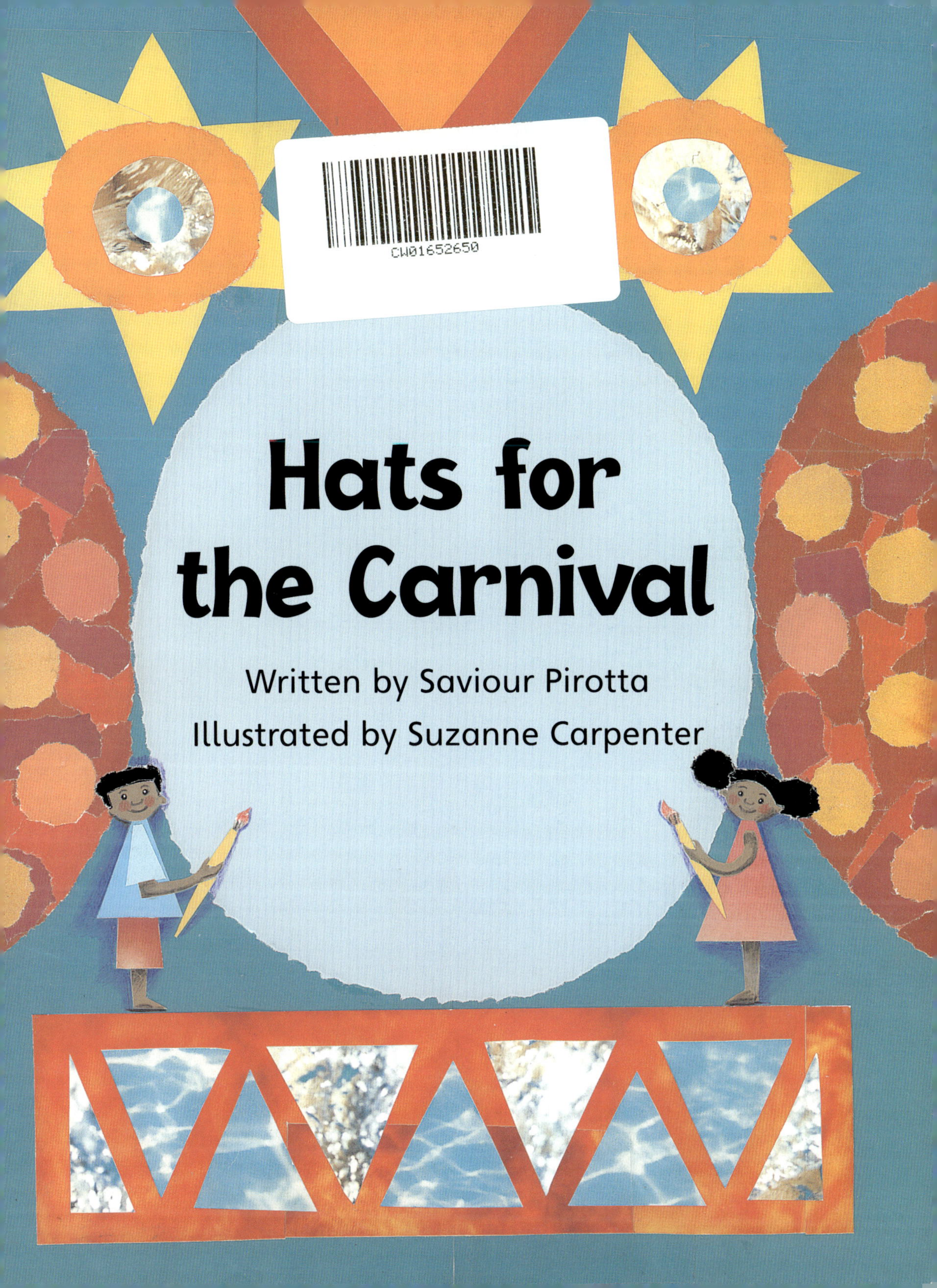



# Hats for the Carnival

Written by Saviour Pirotta
Illustrated by Suzanne Carpenter

It was the day before the carnival. Winston and his friends were trying on their carnival clothes.

"Where are the hats?"
asked Winston.

Just then a man came to the house.
He had some boxes.

“The hats are here,”
said Auntie Doris.

Auntie Doris opened the first box.
It was full of silver paper,
but no hats.

Auntie Doris opened the second box.
It was full of bits of cloth,
but no hats.

Auntie Doris opened the third box.
It was full of thin sticks,
but no hats.

"Oh no! We have got the wrong boxes," she said.
"We have no hats for the carnival."

"Oh no!" said the friends.
"We *must* have hats for the carnival."

Winston thought and thought.

At last he had an idea.
"Come on," he said to his friends.
"Let's get some help."

So all the people in the street helped.
They cut up the silver paper
in the first box.

They painted the cloth
in the second box.

They fixed them to the sticks
in the third box.

Soon there were lots and lots of hats.

"Very good," said Auntie Doris.
"These are the best hats ever!"

The next day Winston and his friends went to the carnival.
They had a good day.

Winston even got a prize
for his carnival hat.

Hooray!